KATE MIDDLETON
AND
PRINCE WILLIAM

KATE MIDDLETON
AND
PRINCE WILLIAM

Angie Timmons

Rosen
YA™

New York

To my prince, Jason—the best husband a woman could ask for

Published in 2020 by The Rosen Publishing Group, Inc.
29 East 21st Street, New York, NY 10010

First Edition

Library of Congress Cataloging-in-Publication Data

Name: Timmons, Angie, author. Title: Kate Middleton and Prince William / Angie Timmons. Description: First edition. | New York: Rosen Publishing, 2020. | Series: Power couples | Includes bibliographical references and index.
Identifiers: LCCN 2018049558 | ISBN 9781508188858 (library bound) | ISBN 9781508188841 (pbk.)
Subjects: LCSH: William, Prince, Duke of Cambridge, 1982– —Juvenile literature. | Catherine, Duchess of Cambridge, 1982– —Juvenile literature. | Royal couples—Great Britain—Biography—Juvenile literature. | Princes—Great Britain—Biography—Juvenile literature. | Princesses—Great Britain—Biography—Juvenile literature.
Classification: LCC DA591.A45 W558446 2020 | DDC 941.086/120922 [B]—dc23
LC record available at https://lccn.loc.gov/2018049558

Manufactured in China

On the cover: Kate Middleton and Prince William, the Duke and Duchess of Cambridge, visit the National Indigenous Training Academy in Yulara, Northern Territory, Australia, in 2014.

CONTENTS

INTRODUCTION

On April 29, 2011, the world watched as Prince William, future king of England and Duke of Cambridge, married his longtime girlfriend, Catherine "Kate" Middleton, the Duchess of Cambridge. According to biographer Kate Shoup, an estimated two billion people worldwide watched the wedding, and one million revelers lined the couple's post-ceremony route between London's Westminster Abbey and Buckingham Palace. Erica Gonzales of *Harper's Bazaar* reported that the wedding cost $34 million in total, with $32 million alone in security expenses.

The wedding day, a Friday, was proclaimed a public holiday in the United Kingdom (Great Britain and Northern Ireland) and its fifty-three Commonwealth countries. Having the day off from work and school, people across Britain celebrated with some five thousand street parties, with thousands of organized celebrations and viewing parties held across the United Kingdom and the Commonwealth.

The wedding was of interest for many reasons. Prince William had dated Middleton for nearly a decade, and public attention to their long courtship was fierce. Their relationship had been documented by the notoriously intrusive British tabloids and globally esteemed news organizations alike.

The April 2011 wedding of Prince William and Kate Middleton was watched by an estimated two billion viewers worldwide. One million people lined the newlywed's procession route between London's Westminster Abbey and Buckingham Palace.

The marriage was also of social and historical interest: per Shoup's biography, it marked the first time in more than 350 years that a direct heir to the British throne married outside the aristocracy (the upper, often noble, class of British society). Middleton was a middle-class girl who had a quiet, happy childhood in the English countryside.

Prince William's life could not have been more different. As the first son of the throne's heir apparent, Prince Charles, William was the subject of intense public interest from the moment he was born. His parents' disastrous marriage and his mother's tragic death in 1997 brought that interest to a fever pitch. When the prince—who many vividly remembered as a grief-stricken teenager at his mother's funeral—showed up as a cheerful groom that sunny spring day in 2011, billions of people worldwide took a personal interest. In the royal son tradition, William joined the military, but he also went above and beyond by signing on for additional service as a search and rescue pilot.

Simply by being royals with high public profiles, many people would consider Prince William and Middleton a power couple. Although fame does often come with power, it's what people do with that power that counts—and the duke and duchess do a great deal. They raise millions of dollars every year that go to charities they run or fund as patrons. The couple often represent the royal family in state visits around the world and are responsible for or expected to attend hundreds of official, social, and ceremonial events each year. Despite their many royal duties, the duke and duchess are hands-on parents to their three young children, who are the future of the British monarchy.

With their unconventional romance and generous spirits, the duke and duchess have endeared themselves to millions. Tasked with the future of the ancient institution of the monarchy, the power couple has ushered in a hopeful new era with a fresh, modern perspective.

CHAPTER 1

MEET PRINCE WILLIAM

Prince William was born June 21, 1982, in London, England. He was the firstborn child of Charles, Prince of Wales, and Lady Diana Spencer, Princess of Wales. William is second in line to the British throne (after his father, Charles) and the grandson of Queen Elizabeth II, the longest-reigning monarch in British history. William has one sibling, his younger brother, Prince Henry (called Harry).

As the son of the long-ruling House of Windsor family, Prince William is a figurehead of the monarchy and has spent his entire life in the public eye. William's

As the firstborn son of the heir to the throne, Prince William (pictured here as a newborn with his mother, Princess Diana, and his father, Prince Charles) has lived his entire life in the public eye.

full name, William Arthur Phillip Louis, reflects the monarchy's long tradition of honoring and carrying on the names of past royals. His titles identify his territorial designations: Duke of Cambridge, Earl of Strathearn, and Baron Carrickfergus.

THE HOUSE OF WINDSOR

William's family, the Windsors, came to power in 1901 when the last House of Hanover monarch, Queen Victoria, died, and her son Edward VII took the throne. The House of Windsor has produced five monarchs, including the current queen, Elizabeth II, who became monarch in 1952.

The family was not known as the Windsors until sixteen years after Victoria's death. Victoria's husband, Prince Albert, came from the German dynasty Saxe-Coburg-Gotha, a name used by Edward VII and his successor George V. However, by the time the third Saxe-Coburg-Gotha monarch, George V, took the throne, World War I (1914–1918) had inspired widespread negative sentiment toward Britain's enemy, Germany. In a public relations move, George V distanced the royals from their Germanic name by proclaiming in 1917 that all Queen Victoria's male descendants would adopt the name Windsor. ("Windsor" derives from Windsor Castle, one of the family's properties.)

Ten years into her reign, Elizabeth II made further modifications to the family name. Elizabeth and her husband, Prince Philip Mountbatten, decreed in 1960 that their descendants would use the hyphenated name Mountbatten-Windsor, with one exception: any royal with the titles "His Royal Highness Prince" or

"Her Royal Highness Princess" isn't legally obligated to use a last name at all, and most don't. Some of the royals use their territorial designations as last names; for instance, when Princes William and Harry served in the British military, they used the last name "Wales" because their father is the Prince of Wales—a title used for the British throne's heir apparent since 1301, when King Edward I of England made a show of power by installing his heir at Caernarfon Castle in Wales. Therefore, Prince William is not known as William Windsor but rather by his royal title and territorial designations.

THE FAMOUS CHILD OF AN INFAMOUS MARRIAGE

William is the son of the current heir to the British throne: Charles, Prince of Wales, Earl of Chester and Carrick, Duke of Cornwall and Rothesay, Baron Renfrew, Lord of the Isles, and Prince and Great Steward of Scotland. Charles was born in 1948 to the present monarch, Queen Elizabeth II, and her husband, Prince Phillip, Duke of Edinburgh. Charles spent his youth in much the usual fashion of a royal heir: private schooling, education in Wales to prepare for his investiture as Prince of Wales, military service with the Royal Navy, and an all-around public figure for Britain. In 1981, he married Lady Diana Frances

In 1981, the wedding of Prince Charles and Diana Spencer was a media event that drew hundreds of millions of viewers. Over the next fifteen years, their unhappy marriage's demise was the source of frequent tabloid headlines.

Spencer (born July 1, 1961, in Norfolk, England) in a globally televised wedding that was, according to the British Broadcasting Company (BBC), watched by hundreds of millions of viewers. William was born in 1982 and his younger brother, Harry, was born two years later.

William attended prestigious schools, including the all-male secondary school, Eton College, founded in 1440 by King Henry VI. He studied art history and geography at the University of St. Andrews, the oldest university in Scotland, after spending a year traveling and volunteering in troubled countries—a sign that he'd picked up his mother's renowned charitable ways.

William's parents had a complicated marriage, which was constant fodder for Britain's notoriously vicious and invasive tabloids. Reports of terrible fights and speculation about infidelities and Diana's alleged eating disorders were headlines around the world. Most notably, while married to Diana, Charles resumed an intimate relationship with Camilla Parker Bowles, whom he had dated in the 1970s. His affair was not a well-kept secret. When Diana and Charles scandalized the world by separating in 1992—with few exceptions over the centuries, British royal marriages did not publicly end—Diana blamed Parker Bowles for the breakup of the marriage.

Parker Bowles grew up in royal circles but was not herself royal, and at the time, members of the royal family were theoretically expected to marry members of the nobility. Diana came from a somewhat humble background; her father was the eighth Earl of Spencer, but her family wasn't especially wealthy or prestigious. However, she hailed from a noble line. She grew up with the queen's youngest sons, Princes Andrew and Edward, and later went to boarding school in Switzerland. Upon returning to England, she became a kindergarten assistant— an unusual career choice for someone from a noble line. She reconnected with the royal family in England, becoming friendly with her future husband in 1980.

William and Harry were conspicuously trapped between their warring parents and between their high-profile public lives and their natural desire just to be children. As they followed in the footsteps of their predecessors—receiving education at the best schools; engaging in traditional sports, pastimes, and public appearances; and preparing for their royal responsibilities—the two boys rarely spent a moment out of the public eye. From their youngest days, the news highlighted the boys in terms of their parents' public dysfunction rather than in terms of their growing involvement in royal duties and their progress as young men.

Diana and Charles remained legally married for four years after their 1992 separation, and they jointly carried out royal duties and raising William and Harry. They finally divorced in 1996. Charles married Parker Bowles in 2005.

Princess Diana was close to her two sons, William (*center*) and Harry, and wanted them to experience life outside the royal bubble. Wherever they went, though, the cameras followed, as seen in this 1990 picture of them vacationing in the Virgin Islands.

THE DIANA DYNAMIC

Throughout her younger years, her marriage, and after her divorce, William's mother, Diana, was involved in many philanthropic efforts. Children's advocacy, AIDS, banning land mines, and support for the arts were just some of the causes for which she used her public profile to raise awareness and funds and to effect change. She was famously pictured holding and feeding starving African children, administering help to AIDS patients, and boldly traversing ground in Angola that was known to have land mines.

Diana was devoted to her sons and to ensuring they grew up to be sensitive, considerate, and charitable young men. She came from a somewhat common (relative to the royal family's) background, which had allowed her to see the world as it really was instead of through the lens of royal privilege. Diana brought William and Harry to visit homeless shelters, orphanages, and hospitals so they could understand suffering. To ensure that they knew the world outside their royal lives, she took the princes to eat at fast food restaurants and sometimes made them ride public transportation.

Diana's way of life and the way she raised her sons earned her the moniker "the People's Princess." She was the unrivaled most popular member of the royal family, even after her divorce. Her popularity resulted in some resentment among the royal family, members of which saw themselves as Britain's rightful

Popular with the public and known for her many charitable works, Diana, pictured here with Princes William and Harry in 1992 at a London-area children's hospital, was affectionately nicknamed the People's Princess.

public figures. Further, Diana's public charity highlighted the lack of such direct, extensive charitable actions among the other royals.

William and Harry were both very close to Diana. William grew to his teenage years in the gulf between his mother, who was largely separate from the royal family, and his life as the future heir to the royal throne. Although Diana and her children were frequently sighted together, in the years leading up to and after her divorce, Diana as an individual became the news because of her public profile, philanthropy, and poise. As Diana dominated the headlines and her divorce from Prince Charles received less attention, William and Harry were, for a few years, able to enjoy relatively peaceful and quiet childhoods.

In August 1997, however, their lives changed forever. While in Scotland with the queen on a traditional royal summer holiday, fifteen-year-old William was suddenly and cruelly catapulted into the public eye.

TRAGIC TEEN YEARS

Diana had long been the subject of intense, intrusive press interest, both at home in England and abroad. The paparazzi hounded her incessantly wherever she went. On August 31, 1997, while attempting to get away from paparazzi who were chasing her car in a tunnel in Paris, France, Diana was killed in a car accident. Her boyfriend, Dodi Fayed, and their driver, Henri Paul, also died in the crash.

Many blamed Diana's death on the paparazzi's incessant hounding. (In 2008, a British inquest jury found both Paul and the paparazzi guilty of the accident.) Photos captured just before the crash showed the princess looking anxiously out the car's back window at the multiple paparazzi-filled cars in pursuit.

The world was rocked by Diana's death. Per the BBC, two thousand people, including multiple celebrities and dignitaries, filled London's Westminster Abbey for her funeral, and an estimated 2.5 billion people around the world watched on television. Hundreds of thousands of mourners lined London's streets to watch the funeral procession. Thousands of flowers piled up outside Kensington Palace, a royal residence where Diana had retained an apartment and offices.

(continued on the next page)

Princes William (*left*) and Harry (*second from right*) follow Princess Diana's coffin during her funeral procession. They walk alongside Prince Charles (*right*) and their uncle Earl Spencer.

(continued from the previous page)

The world watched as William and Harry walked, heads down, behind their mother's hearse. (Harry later revealed that Charles had ordered them not to cry.) Queen Elizabeth's unemotional demeanor throughout the funeral sparked public outrage, and the royal family became the subject of intense criticism from a public that faulted its members for years of emotionally abusing Diana.

William was stuck in a world of tension: among the royal family, between the royals and the Spencers, and between the royals and the public. Expected to carry out his royal responsibilities without disruption, William showed remarkable resilience—only years later would he publicly discuss his mother's death.

Time makes it easier. I know how you feel. I still miss my mother every day—and it's 20 years after she died."
—PRINCE WILLIAM

William has carried on Diana's legacy. He's involved in multiple charities and openly espouses his respect for his mother's charitable work. POPSUGAR reported that during a 2016 visit to a hospice center, William told a fourteen-year-old boy who was grieving the loss of his mother that he understood the boy's grief. "Time makes it easier. I know how you feel. I still miss my mother every day—and it's 20 years after she died."

POWERFUL PEERS

In the many centuries in which travel was confined to horses, carriages, and walking, monarchs would sometimes go years without visiting the more distant reaches of their kingdoms. Therefore, nobles such as dukes, earls, and barons—most of whom shared blood with the monarch—were entrusted with ruling over their titular territories (for example, the Duke of Northumberland oversaw the vast northern territory of Northumberland) for the monarch. These nobles administered justice, enforced laws, collected taxes and incomes, trained soldiers, and served as high-ranking military officials. Many nobles became powerful rulers. Some were richer than the monarch and had strong claims to the throne. Many historic European civil wars were caused by powerful nobles who rebelled against the throne, which was commonly held by a member of their own families. Most notably in England, in the fifteenth century, Edward, Duke of York, rebelled against his cousin, the Lancastrian King Henry VI, with the powerful Earl of Warwick in a civil war called the Wars of the Roses. (This war inspired the book *A Song of Ice and Fire* by George R. R. Martin and the TV show *Game of Thrones*.) Edward won the throne in 1471. Edward and his wife, Elizabeth, gave birth to the Tudor dynasty, a royal line with which the Windsors of today share a direct blood line.

(continued on the next page)

(continued from the previous page)

British peers still hold their titles (most are inherited, along with their historic properties), but they don't possess the power of their ancestors and predecessors, who led battles during war, often inspired the loyalty of those people who lived in their territories, and rivaled the monarchy in power. Today, they enjoy social influence and prestige, but their real power has declined along with the monarchy's. Since Parliament's first rebellions against the monarchy and nobility in the seventeenth century, both historical institutions have receded into mostly ceremonial functions.

WILLIAM'S NOBLE TITLES

Like his predecessors' titles throughout the centuries, William's titles reflect royal investiture—the practice of formally giving someone specific honors or ranks. Investiture is a practice of a historic royal legal system called peerage that encompasses hereditary titles and noble ranks bestowed on those who swear loyalty to the Crown in exchange for land or money. The United Kingdom's peerage system encompasses Great Britain (England, Northern Ireland, Scotland, and Wales) and used to come with potent political power: peers' birthrights allowed them to sit in the British Parliament's upper house, the House of Lords. However, a 1999 law ousted most of the Parliament's peers.

The Duke of Cambridge is a title that dates to the seventeenth century and is named after the English city of Cambridge. In most of Europe, dukes are usually monarchs or members of a royal family that rules over a duchy, a territory or geopolitical region. Dukes are usually the highest-ranking nobles after the monarch. In the United Kingdom's peerage system, dukes rule over royal dukedoms—titles and territories created for members of the royal family. William's earldom and barony titles reflect another long-running British royal tradition of bestowing rule over specific territories to members of the royal family and other nobility.

In William's case, his earldom and barony indicate Britain's historic power over neighboring nations. The Earl of Strathearn is an ancient Scottish investiture that dates to the twelfth century and reflects England's dominion over its northern neighbor. The title Baron Carrickfergus dates to the mid-nineteenth century and refers to the Northern Irish town of Carrickfergus; Northern Ireland remained a part of Britain after much of Ireland successfully revolted against the British monarchy and formed the Republic of Ireland in the early twentieth century.

William's titles were bestowed upon him by his grandmother, Queen Elizabeth II, on his wedding day in 2011. His wife, Princess Catherine "Kate" Elizabeth Middleton, became the Duchess of Cambridge, the Countess of Strathearn, and Lady Carrickfergus.

CHAPTER 2

MEET KATE

Catherine "Kate" Elizabeth Middleton was born on January 8, 1982, in Reading, England. Her parents, Carole and Michael Middleton, met while working for British Airways. Carole was a flight attendant, and Michael was a steward and a dispatcher. Kate mostly grew up in the southeastern English county of Berkshire, which, despite being close to the metropolitan area of London, is known for its many picturesque, rural areas. Between 1984 and 1986, the Middletons lived in the Arabian country of Jordan as part of Michael's job with British Airways. Kate attended an English-speaking nursery school in Jordan.

Kate Middleton, pictured here at age three on a family vacation in England's Lake District, had a very different childhood from that of her husband: happy, middle class, and, as a nonroyal, out of the public eye.

Kate is the oldest of three children. Her sister, Philippa "Pippa" Charlotte Middleton, was born in 1983, and her brother, James William Middleton, was born in 1987.

A "COMMON" GIRL DESTINED FOR AN UNCOMMON LIFE

By English society standards, Kate's family was "common," a term used to describe people who don't come from noble families. Though Kate's parents eventually achieved enough wealth to raise them into the ranks of the upper class, her ancestry is a mixed bag, and several of her ancestors came from very humble beginnings indeed.

Unlike most of Prince William's family members, Kate's mother, Carole, didn't have family money and she didn't come close to descending from the British noble and upper class. When she became an adult, she had to earn a living, and she became a flight attendant for British Airways. This path was a seemingly unremarkable decision and an ordinary enough job. Her career choice, however, would change the course of British history.

THE MIDDLETONS OF LEEDS

Kate's father, Michael Middleton, born in the northern English city of Leeds, came from a much higher social class than his wife, Carole. Michael's family wasn't nobility, but its members had some measure of wealth and prestige; dating back almost two hundred years, the Middletons had a long-running law firm in Leeds and some aristocratic connections.

"FROM PIT TO PALACE"

In the nineteenth century and the first half of the twentieth century, thousands of working-class people in England toiled in the country's notoriously grim coal mines. Although the coal mines generated great wealth for those who owned and operated them, the miners—who generally came from poor backgrounds— were exposed to extremely harsh and dangerous conditions deep in the coal pits that were gouged into large areas of the country.

One of these coal miners was Kate's maternal great great-grandfather, John Harrison, who came from a long line of coal miners. When Kate and Prince William were engaged to be married and it became clear that Kate would one day be queen, British tabloids dug into her family's humble coal-mining background under the headline "From Pit to Palace." (The tabloids' persistent mockery of Kate's "common" background eerily echoed the press treatment Princess Diana endured in the 1980s, when Diana's noble but not particularly prestigious background was mocked as being "common.")

(continued on the next page)

(continued from the previous page)

John Harrison's son, Thomas Harrison (Kate's great-grandfather), wasn't keen to follow in the family tradition. He took up carpentry and moved his family to London in the 1940s, seeking a better life away from his coal-mining hometown. (Thomas Harrison's daughter Dorothy was Carole's mother and Kate's grandmother.)

The family stayed in the London area but didn't exactly achieve the non-coal-mining success Thomas Harrison sought. Kate's mother, Carole, was raised on a council estate (a form of British public housing) in the London area.

Michael's father, Peter Francis Middleton, didn't follow his ancestors into law. He was a captain in the Royal Air Force and served Britain as a fighter pilot in World War II. Like most of his ancestors, Peter Middleton attended the prestigious Oxford University (a tradition from which Kate's father, Michael, broke when he opted to go to flight school instead). Michael Middleton's mother, Valerie, was a World War II hero in her own right: she was a member of the code-breaking team that deciphered secret communications between England's World War II enemies. Even with these esteemed records, Kate's paternal grandparents only scratch the surface of a prominent family with ties to England's history.

A POLITICAL PRECEDENT

Codebreakers at Bletchley Park deciphered coded communications between Adolf Hitler and his military during World War II. Kate Middleton's paternal grandmother, Valerie, was part of the codebreaking team at Bletchley Park.

Kate's marriage into the British royal family is not the first time someone from her bloodline rose to political prominence. When Kate's great-grandfather Richard Noel Middleton, a lawyer, wed Olive Lupton in 1914, he married into a family with a long history of political achievements and connections.

KATE'S ARISTOCRATIC HERITAGE

Through her great-grandmother Olive Middleton (née Lupton), Kate's Middleton side of the family has political and aristocratic associations, and even royal associations dating back to the first Tudor king in the fifteenth century. Olive Middleton was cousin to a baroness and herself moved in aristocratic circles. (Incidentally, Olive's brother Lionel was a classmate of Princess Diana's grandfather Albert Spencer, the seventh Earl of Spencer, at the University of Cambridge.)

Olive's family, the Luptons, rose to academic and religious prominence in the sixteenth century. Roger Lupton, an administrator at Eton College in Berkshire, was chaplain to two Tudor kings, Henry VII and Henry VIII, in the late fifteenth and early sixteenth centuries. The Lupton name first appears in public records in seventeenth-century Leeds. The earliest-mentioned Lupton was a minister, indicating the family continued in the religious tradition set forth by Roger Lupton. (An eighteenth-century Lupton, William II, also became a minister.) These early religious connections were important in a country where religion was very much intertwined with politics.

Starting in at least the seventeenth century, the Luptons were farmers and wool manufacturers with trading connections in mainland Europe. Over the next couple of centuries, the Luptons rose to great prominence in Leeds, where several nineteenth- and early twentieth-century Luptons served as Lord

Mayor. The family contributed its wealth to civic and educational needs and became involved in British politics; in fact, one Arnold Lupton was elected to Parliament in 1906. The Lupton family's commercial and political successes led to its reputation as "a political and business dynasty," according to a nineteenth-century entry in the Leeds city archives.

DISTANTLY NOBLE

The British tabloids' initial assessment of Kate's "common" background was proven to be technically inaccurate when

Gilling Castle in North Yorkshire, England, is pictured here before 1939. Middleton shares descent from Sir Thomas Fairfax with Prince William. The Fairfax base was Gilling Castle.

research revealed some interesting ancestry. Through one of his Lupton cousins, Kate's father is connected to an eighteenth-century marquess (a British nobleman that ranks lower than a duke but higher than an earl). Through the Middletons directly, Kate shares distant relatives with her husband: Sir Thomas Fairfax and his wife, Anne Gascoigne, who was descended from a fourteenth-century king of England, Edward III. Because the marquess connection is not through her direct Middleton line and because Anne Gascoigne did not hold a noble title that was passed down, Kate's noble and royal ancestry was obscured over the centuries.

THE EARLY DAYS

Though some of Kate's ancestors were prestigious, she was not born into an aristocratic life. By the time her parents met, English societal expectations for marriage had changed a great deal since the peak days of the aristocratic Luptons. People from upper-class backgrounds, like Kate's father, were not so widely expected to marry up or within their social class to maintain class distinction and wealth. Free to marry someone of his choice, he married Carole Goldsmith, a working-class girl.

Kate's parents made a living through their work at British Airways. By the time Kate turned ten, however, things had changed. After her brother, James, was born, her mother started Party Pieces, a mail-order

children's party planning business that ultimately did very well. Michael eventually was able to quit British Airways and work full time for Party Pieces. The British press has at times

The Middleton family's party planning business, Party Pieces, has at times been criticized as too tacky to be associated with the royal family. However, its success has made Kate Middleton a wealthy heiress.

ridiculed the Middletons' business, considering it too tacky to be associated with the royal family. However, Party Pieces's success is ultimately responsible for the Middletons' ability to send Kate to the respected educational institutions that lined her path to meeting the future king of England.

AN UPPER-MIDDLE-CLASS UPBRINGING

When the Middletons returned to England from Jordan in 1986, Michael and Carole enrolled Kate in a local school. After their party planning business took off, though, Kate began to live the typical life of a child from an upper-middle-class English family. The Middletons moved into a larger home, and Kate left her local school to move on to prestigious boarding and day schools in

The Middleton family's success allowed Kate (*front row, left*) to attend well-respected educational institutions, like St. Andrew's Preparatory School. As a ten-year-old, Kate first saw Prince William when his school's hockey team visited St. Andrew's.

Berkshire. She first attended St. Andrew's Preparatory School. As reported in the *Telegraph*, it was at St. Andrew's that ten-year-old Kate first laid eyes on her future husband, when nine-year-old Prince William visited with his boarding school's hockey team. Kate was one of many young St. Andrew's schoolgirls fighting to

> I was lucky. My parents and teachers provided me with a wonderful and secure childhood where I always knew I was loved, valued, and listened to."
>
> **–KATE MIDDLETON**

catch a glimpse of the future king, but she wouldn't see him up close until they officially met at college years later. After St. Andrew's, Kate moved on to two well-respected preparatory institutions, Downe House School and Marlborough College (a secondary school similar to high school), all in Berkshire.

Kate was a good student (she liked school so much that when she was young, she wanted to be a teacher) and a good athlete. Newer to her wealth and status than some of her classmates, Kate was generally shy and modest. She was close to her family, especially her sister, Pippa, who was only a year younger than Kate.

By all accounts, including her own, Kate had a happy childhood in the idyllic Berkshire countryside: "I was lucky. My parents and teachers provided me with a wonderful and secure childhood where I always knew I was loved, valued, and listened to," she said in a 2015 speech. The Middletons' non-noble status allowed them the flexibility to be easygoing and warm, a contrast to the often-strict rules imposed on members of the royal family to maintain public appearances. The family's wealth afforded Kate and Pippa the ability to travel, receive good educations, and associate with members of high society.

After graduating from Marlborough College, Kate, like Prince William, did not go directly to college, opting instead to take a gap year. During that time, she traveled and developed her interest in art—another thing she would ultimately have in common with the prince. Thanks to her relaxed upbringing, the reminders of her family's humbler roots, and the advantages her parents' recent wealth had provided her, Kate grew to be a thoughtful, responsible young woman. She exhibited good sense and poise, traits that would one day serve her well in her very public role.

A child of the English countryside, Kate opted to go to a university that was far from the hustle and bustle of London or other large cities. She chose the University of St. Andrews in Scotland. In 2001, she moved into one of the university's coeducational residence halls, St. Salvatore's (nicknamed "Sally's"), at the same time as Prince William. It was here that Kate's quiet, peaceful life would transform forever.

CHAPTER 3

A ROYAL ROMANCE

For more than 150 years, members of the royal family have gone to college at Oxford or Cambridge. Prince William did not intend to follow in this tradition. Instead, the young prince wished to attend school at faraway St. Andrews in Scotland.

Prince Charles had concerns. Oxford and Cambridge were arguably better equipped to handle a royal student, and their proximities to London would enable the royal family to quickly respond to any incidents.

Prince William, pictured here with his father on his first day of college in 2001, convinced the royal family to allow him to attend the University of St. Andrews in Scotland instead of Oxford or Cambridge, the traditional university choices for British royals.

Prince William made his case: he wanted as ordinary a college life as he could get before he had to assume his role as a royal figurehead, and he believed St. Andrews was the place where that could happen. Prince Charles finally agreed. The royal family renewed its agreement with the press, asking the media to leave William alone at college in exchange for regular updates about him. In September 2001, William moved in to Sally's, upstairs from Kate Middleton's room.

A FRIENDSHIP GROWS

Prince William was happy to arrive at St. Andrews, far from the daily rigors of royal life. The shy country girl Kate Middleton was named the prettiest girl at Sally's by the end of their first week at St. Andrews, but that did not affect her modest ways, which intrigued William—she was a sharp contrast to the multiple young women who went out of their way to try to get his attention. The prince and Middleton bonded over common interests, like their travels during their gap years, art, and sports. Within a couple months, Middleton and the prince had established a good friendship, but nothing more. Prince William had a fleeting romantic relationship with another University of St. Andrews student, Carley Massy-Birch, during his first semester at the university. This relationship ended when Massy-Birch gave him an ultimatum:

he had to decide between her and a high-society girl, Arabella Musgrave, whom he frequently saw on visits home. Although he seemed to choose Musgrave, his relationship with her fizzled out, too.

CATCHING A PRINCE'S EYE

The Kate Middleton whom Prince William first met at St. Andrews was beautiful, but she was a Berkshire country girl who loved sports and the outdoors more than fashion and makeup. William had shown a friendly interest in her during their time at St. Andrews, but he pursued romantic relationships with other young women. In a November 16, 2010, interview with the UK Press Association, William explained his early days as Middleton's friend: "When I first met Kate I knew there was something very special about her. I knew there was possibly something that I wanted to explore there. We ended up being friends for a while and that just sort of was a good foundation. Because I do generally believe now that being friends with one another is a massive advantage."

His interest grew rapidly one fateful spring evening. According to Sarah Grossbart of E!News, on March 27, 2002, when Middleton strutted down the catwalk in a see-through black dress at St. Andrews's annual

(continued on the next page)

At a 2002 charity fashion show, Prince William saw his friend Kate Middleton in a new light when she strutted down the catwalk in a see-through dress. The now-famous dress was sold at auction in 2011 for $125,000.

(continued from the previous page)

student-run charity fashion show, the prince was thoroughly impressed. He reportedly turned to a friend and exclaimed, "Kate's hot!"

At the time, Middleton was dating another St. Andrews student. This situation did not prevent Prince William from pursuing her at the fashion show's after-party, where he engaged her in deep conversation. As Grossbart later reported, Middleton was shocked when he tried to kiss her, pulling away from him in a room full of curious onlookers. She blushed at the compliments he poured on her, and witnesses said it was clear she was the same level-headed, conscientious Kate Middleton they knew from before her daring catwalk debut. The most eligible bachelor in England was going to have to put in time and effort if he was going to win her heart.

A CONFLICTED YOUNG MAN

Partially through his first semester at college, the nineteen-year-old prince's enthusiasm for his life at St. Andrews waned. He found himself torn between the laid-back college life he'd been so determined to have and the excitement and familiarity of London and Gloucester (a part of England where he'd spent much of his childhood).

At Christmas, he informed his father he did not want to return to St. Andrews. So far, life at college hadn't turned out how he'd wanted. "I don't think I was homesick; I was more daunted," the prince told biographer Katie Nicholl.

Prince Charles convinced his son to return to St. Andrews for at least one semester. This time around, he made more friends, and the students rallied around him to make him feel more at home. As the semester progressed, he found another reason to stick around in Scotland.

ROOMING WITH A ROYAL

The March 2002 fashion show came and went, the spring semester ended, and the St. Andrews students left for the summer. Despite the prince's romantic interest in Middleton, the two supposedly remained just friends. The prince had demanded he be allowed to live off campus his second year, and when the students returned to St. Andrews for the fall 2002 semester, he moved into an apartment with three of his friends, including Middleton. He took great joy in sharing ordinary household duties and an ordinary life with his roommates (after, of course, the bullet-proof glass and windows and other security precautions required for a prince's dwelling were installed). In her biography on the royal couple, Nicholl wrote, "It was a luxury no prince before him had enjoyed and exactly the normalcy he craved."

Middleton and Prince William were roommates during college. They managed to keep a low profile until a photographer snapped a photo of them on a ski trip in 2004.

According to a November 4, 2010, article by Nicholl in *Vanity Fair*, Middleton and her royal roommate insisted they were still only friends, though those closest to them knew that wasn't the case. By summer 2003, they'd fallen in love, but because of his royal status and the attention a public romance would attract, they took great pains to appear they weren't romantically involved. It would be nearly another year before their relationship was made public.

THE ROCKY ROAD TO ROYAL ROMANCE

When Middleton and William returned to St. Andrews in the fall of 2003, they moved into a private estate away from the center of town. They enjoyed the estate's privacy, which allowed them to do things like hold hands and have picnics. Although the people at St. Andrews were aware of their relationship, the two had seemingly managed to keep their romance away from the attention of the media.

"WAITY KATIE"

In the summer of 2004, William and Middleton broke up. This separation was the first of several high-profile splits the couple would go through in their on-again, off-again romance. The couple's bumpy, twisting, decade-long road to the altar caused the press to nickname Middleton "Waity Katie."

When Middleton and William graduated from St. Andrews in June 2005, their future seemed unclear. William's graduation meant he was going to have to get serious about his royal responsibilities, such

Kate Middleton (*left*) and Prince William (*right*) graduated from college in June 2005. His graduation marked the end of the quiet life the prince had enjoyed in college and the beginning of a life of royal duty and public service.

as representing the queen on official state visits overseas. Amid widespread speculation that he would soon propose to Middleton, William went another way entirely.

A PRESSING ISSUE

The couple's sacred privacy came to an end in April 2004, when the British newspaper the *Sun* published a photo of the loving couple on a ski trip in Switzerland. The royal family was livid that the newspaper had broken the agreement to leave the prince alone during his school years. The royals' relationship with the press was a sensitive issue following Diana's fatal race to escape the paparazzi. Unfortunately, there was nothing the royals or Middleton could do. The secret was out, and the press pounced on the shy Berkshire country girl.

Middleton handled the attention with unexpected grace. Wanting to avoid a repeat of Princess Diana's difficult adjustment to life in the spotlight, the royal family eventually arranged for Middleton to be trained for the public spotlight. With their romance public, William and Middleton were increasingly sighted out and about. They spent time with each other's families and their friends, and Middleton's sister, Pippa, began joining them on trips and weekend getaways.

The couple endured their early days in the public spotlight with poise. However, like most young relationships, the couple hit rough patches. During one particularly rough patch, Middleton had to involve lawyers after the press ignored her family's pleas to leave them alone at their Berkshire home, where reporters and photographers had taken up position in an unrelenting attempt to get an interview. It wouldn't be the last time the couple had to get stern with the media, which showed a keen interest in hounding Middleton about her relationship with the prince.

ROYAL RESPONSIBILITIES

At age twenty-three, William decided it was time to meet his royal obligation of military service. In January 2006, he headed off to military training for forty-four weeks. The prince grew more aggressive in denying his plans to marry Middleton, but he still invited her and her parents to his military training graduation in December 2006. This step seemed to indicate that Middleton was going to be the next queen of England, and the press followed her constantly. However, William increasingly distanced himself from Middleton beginning in early 2007, leading them to break up again over Easter weekend.

THIS TIME FOR GOOD

Middleton prevailed despite hurtful commentary, like her being too middle class to marry a prince, that circulated through her social circles and the press after her breakup with William. She trained for an arduous rowing trip across the English Channel with friends and was regularly seen out on the town, enjoying London's epic nightlife. What almost no one knew was that William and Middleton were already back together. Their breakup had proven they were still very much in love. This time, they stayed together for good, even weathering William's additional military training, which he started in the fall of 2008 after spending the summer with the Royal Navy.

In January 2006, Prince William trained to be a search-and-rescue pilot with the Royal Air Force. His decision to pursue further military service rather than marry and settle into his other royal duties shocked many.

LONG-DISTANCE LOVE

William shocked everyone with his decision to pursue further military service because it meant postponing the next phase of his princely duties, which included deep involvement in philanthropic work and a greater role as a royal figure. To balance their military and charity work, Harry and William set up their own household and combined their charity endeavors. This combined effort quickly resulted in the two princes heading and funding multiple charities. In a quote from Nicholl's biography, William said he and his younger brother were made to understand at a young age "that with these great privileges goes an absolute responsibility to give back."

> **[I and Harry understood as children] that with these great privileges goes an absolute responsibility to give back."**
>
> **—PRINCE WILLIAM**

William's military training also meant that he and Middleton spent most of 2009 and 2010 apart. However, she spent that time settling in with the royal family, becoming a regular guest at members' functions and being hosted at their various estates. When Middleton and William were able to spend time together, they clearly relished it. They settled into a happy, hopeful relationship, with their eyes focused on the conclusion of William's military training and the future beyond that.

CHAPTER 4

A POWER COUPLE IS CREATED

By the fall of 2010, Middleton and Prince William had been dating for eight years. Their endurance over the years had proven their love—and hinted they were strong enough to face the biggest challenge yet: tying the knot and preparing for life as the future British monarchs.

THE BIG MOMENT

In October 2010, while on a trip to Kenya, Prince William finally proposed to his longtime girlfriend, Kate Middleton. She said yes.

The royal family officially announced the prince's engagement in November 2010. Anticipation for the royal wedding reached a fever pitch around the world. Parallels were drawn to the media event from thirty years earlier, when Prince Charles married Diana.

William proposed with his mother's engagement ring as a symbolic way to involve the late princess in one of the biggest days of his life. The press went wild, and observers of the couple's long relationship rejoiced. The royal family's planning for the wedding day kicked into high gear. Prince Charles's 1981 wedding to Princess Diana had been watched by millions around the world; with the advent of new technologies in the thirty years that had passed, even more people around the world would be able to watch Prince William's wedding. The royal family couldn't disappoint. Anticipation for the big day was feverish, with near-daily updates about the couple and their wedding plans.

THE ROYAL WEDDING: A WORLDWIDE SPECTACLE

Just two months shy of the thirty-year anniversary of his parents' wedding day, Prince William married Kate Middleton at Westminster Abbey in the media global event of 2011. Prince Harry served as best man, and Pippa as maid of honor. About 1,900 guests attended. The day, April 29, was a public holiday in Britain, and people from around the world descended on London to line the streets for the wedding procession, which included traditional aspects like the bride and

(continued on the next page)

(continued from the previous page)

groom's open-air carriage ride from Westminster Abbey to Buckingham Palace, where they followed the tradition of appearing on the balcony to greet the crowd. Tens of millions of people around the world watched the nearly four-hour event on television. According to Google, another seventy-two million watched live on YouTube. (The entire video can still be viewed on YouTube.) After the ceremony, Westminster Abbey's ten bells rang a full peal, lasting more than three hours.

Middleton arrived for her wedding at London's Westminster Abbey with her sister and maid of honor, Pippa Middleton. The abbey's bells rang for more than three hours after the new Duke and Duchess of Cambridge wed.

Middleton's wedding ring is made of Welsh gold, a nearly one-hundred-year-old tradition for British royal wedding rings. Prince William did not choose to get a wedding ring, but he looked every part the royal groom in his military uniform. The stunning bride wore a striking but simple designer gown (created by Sarah Burton at Alexander McQueen), while several female members of the royal family appeared in elaborate hats and fascinators. The media coverage that lasted long after the ceremony ended dissected everything from what the wedding guests wore to the more traditional, historical features of the wedding day.

On the morning of the wedding, the royal family announced that, following the royal practice of granting titles upon marriage to royal princes, William was to be become Duke of Cambridge, Earl of Strathearn, and Baron Carrickfergus. Middleton became Her Royal Highness The Duchess of Cambridge after the wedding.

RULES OF "THE FIRM"

Now married and officially the Duke and Duchess of Cambridge, William and Middleton were expected to enter the full scope of their public lives as figureheads in the world's most famous family. "The Firm," as the royal family refers to itself, is guided by strict rules that generally come down from the queen herself.

The rules are intended to aid royal family members in their official capacities and in their public lives, in everything from behavior (such as who's expected to curtsy to the queen) to expectations for charity work. The rulebook was revised when Prince Charles married his longtime mistress, Camilla Parker Bowles, in 2005, and again when William and Kate wed in 2011.

ADJUSTING TO NEW REALITIES

Like Middleton, Parker Bowles was not herself royal or noble, meaning a fair amount of official introduction into the responsibilities of her social and legal elevation was in order. Rulebook revisions were also necessitated by the scandalous and unpopular history of her relationship with Charles. The queen wanted the royal family to be prepared to answer press questions and be informed on coexisting with her in public, such as who gets pride of place next to the queen at official state functions and who stands where in photographs.

Although Middleton's relationship with Prince William was nowhere near as controversial as that of Prince Charles and Parker Bowles, it had, nonetheless, been a long and bumpy courtship, and she came from a middle-class (albeit wealthy) family. To get everyone in the family on the same page about how to discuss Middleton and how to treat her in public and private, as well as to educate Middleton herself on life as a royal, the queen's rules were updated when the prince got married.

The queen has been forced to accept the reality of her heirs' choices in non-noble, nonroyal spouses over the last few decades (though her distaste is sometimes shown in her own quiet way—for instance, she did not attend her son Charles's wedding to Parker Bowles in 2005, and her dislike for her son's longtime love is well known). She's shown a measured acceptance to changes in the typically rigid royal structure. However, Queen Elizabeth II's rules and her public conduct prove she takes her family's role on the worldwide stage seriously and maintains traditional notions and often strict expectations for herself and her family. Because of this standard, Middleton was put through rigorous training to handle public attention and train for life as a royal, and she's often applauded for her public poise and the respect she shows for the ancient institution into which she married.

A GRACEFUL TIME

As the future sovereigns (supreme rulers), the duke and duchess faced the traditional pressure to begin producing heirs and carrying out their many charitable, official, and ceremonial duties. However, the queen took to heart the complaints of the late Princess Diana, who had felt like an outsider among the royal family, left to fend for herself with the incessant press attention. In addition to the training Middleton received to handle public life as a royal,

After their wedding, the Duke and Duchess of Cambridge quietly settled into married life on the Welsh island of Anglesey. They did perform some royal duties, such as making state visits like this one to Canada in July 2011.

the queen went a step further to ensure the couple had an easy transition. After their wedding, she granted the new duke and duchess a two-year grace period in which their royal expectations were relaxed, giving them time to enjoy the early years of their marriage. The couple spent this time living in a farmhouse on the Welsh island of Anglesey, near where the duke was serving as a pilot with the Royal Air Force.

> It was such a special time for us. It was the start of our life together really."
>
> —KATE MIDDLETON

During their grace period, the newlyweds really did take advantage of the break from public life and expectations. Except for a housecleaner and the requisite royal bodyguards, they didn't have the usual army of servants that attend to the royal family in their palaces. They cooked their own meals, shopped for their own groceries, walked their dog, and stayed in watching DVDs most nights. According to a February 18, 2016, *Telegraph* article about the couple's return to Anglesey for an event, the duchess fondly remembered the early years of their marriage on the island: "It was such a special time for us. It was the start of our life together really."

The couple did swiftly meet one important royal expectation during their grace period: Middleton became pregnant with the couple's first child in 2012. Prince George of Cambridge was born on July 22, 2013, in London.

The Duke and Duchess of Cambridge are seen here with their three children: Prince George (born in 2013 and third in line to the throne), Princess Charlotte (born in 2015), and Prince Louis (born in 2018).

A POWER COUPLE IS CREATED

AN HEIR AND TWO SPARES

Dating back to ancient times, members of dynastic families—like Britain's royal family—have been expected to secure their future power through heirs. Before modern medicine, members of ruling classes were under particular pressure to produce multiple heirs because of the many health dangers faced by expectant mothers, young children, and adults alike. Having at least two children in line to inherit power has been jokingly called "an heir and spare," a reference to producing an additional child to step in, in case the first heir died.

The Duke and Duchess of Cambridge have done their heir duty. Their firstborn, Prince George Alexander Louis of Cambridge, is third in line for the throne after his father and grandfather. On May 2, 2015, the royal family welcomed George's little sister, Princess Charlotte Elizabeth Diana of Cambridge. On April 23, 2018, the Duchess of Cambridge gave birth to a second son, Prince Louis Arthur Charles of Cambridge.

A MODERN-ISH MONARCHY

When Prince George was due to be born in 2013, the British monarchy pushed forth the Succession to the Crown Act to modernize the practice of inheriting the throne. The act permits firstborn daughters to inherit

(continued on the next page)

(continued from the previous page)

the throne, removing more than a thousand years of primogeniture (a legal precedent granting male heirs the right to inherit the throne). Queen Elizabeth II only succeeded to the throne because her father, King George VI, had no male heirs. If she'd had brothers, even younger brothers, they would have succeeded to the throne instead of her.

The history of British succession is complicated and sometimes sinister. The infamous King Henry VIII, who reigned from 1509 to 1547, divorced or beheaded several wives who failed to produce male heirs. He forced England's separation from the Catholic Church and founded his own church, the Protestant Church of England, so he could divorce and remarry when a wife failed to give birth to a boy. His nine-year-old son, Edward VI, succeeded to the throne despite having two older sisters from Henry VIII's first and second wives. Edward VI's death at the age of fifteen threw the country into chaos as multiple claimants to the throne battled for rule.

British succession is also governed by religion. Starting with Henry VIII and to this day, only Protestants can inherit the throne. Prior to the passage of an amendment to the 2013 succession act that allows heirs to the throne to marry Catholics, heirs who married Catholics had to forfeit their right to the throne.

The British monarchy is an old, complex institution that moves slowly in modernizing its practices. However, the introduction of nonroyals into the royal family, such as Middleton and Prince Harry's American wife, Meghan Markle, signifies that the next generation of British royals doesn't intend to adhere to old-fashioned laws and traditions.

LITTLE CHILDREN, BIG TITLES

William and Middleton's children bear "of Cambridge" at the end of their names because their parents are the Duke and Duchess of Cambridge. Before Princess Charlotte was born, the queen decreed that all of Prince William's children, not just his firstborn, would be officially recognized by the royal titles of "prince" or "princess." The queen's decree also dictated that the title of "royal highness" would be given to all of Prince William's children; therefore, Princes George and Louis are "His Royal Highnesses" and Princess Charlotte is "Her Royal Highness." Members of the royal family, even direct heirs to the throne, are not born with the royal highness titles; the title is granted by decree of the reigning sovereign. Thanks to the succession act initiated in 2013 and finalized in 2015, Princess Charlotte is the first-ever female royal to officially secure her place in line for the British throne.

Like royal children before them, the three royal children are the subjects of great public interest. The press camped outside the hospitals when Middleton was admitted for extreme morning sickness and when she went into labor. The announcements of their births were splashed across front pages around the world and reported on extensively. The press often photographs them, and the public enjoys regular updates on their milestones, such as starting school. The duke and duchess have given the children space to enjoy childhood, and the three young royal children are occasionally spotted playing or getting up to ordinary childhood mischief.

Unlike many royal parents in the past, the duke and duchess are affectionate, devoted parents who appear to model their child-rearing more after how Middleton was raised than the way Prince William was raised, resulting in more hands-on parenting and more publicly affectionate relationships with their children. In fact, when George was born, after the requisite stop to be presented to his great-grandmother, the queen, the duke and duchess promptly brought their newborn to Middleton's childhood Berkshire country home—away from the public spotlight.

Still, the three children will be expected to follow in the footsteps of the royals who came before them. They will likely be sent to prestigious boarding schools like their father and grandfather before them. From an early age, they will take their places at official state functions and be expected to follow the rules of "the Firm."

CHAPTER 5

ROYAL REALITIES

I n February 2017, at the age of ninety, Queen Elizabeth II celebrated her Sapphire Jubilee. She's the first-ever British monarch to reach the milestone, which commemorates sixty-five years on the throne; in September 2015, she surpassed her great-great grandmother Victoria as the longest-reigning monarch.

British sovereigns (kings and queens) reign for life. When Queen Elizabeth II dies, her heir apparent, Charles, the Prince of Wales, will assume the throne, and William, Duke of Cambridge, will become his heir apparent and inherit the throne when Charles dies.

CONSORTING WITH ROYALTY

People often wonder why Prince Philip, husband to Queen Elizabeth II, is not called king. It's because of a very old style of recognizing the spouses of kings and queens as "consorts," who share their spouses' rank and status but are not regnants (sovereigns who rule in their own right because they were born into the reigning royal family or legally inherited the throne, like Queen Elizabeth II).

Prince Philip is a king consort, though he does not use it as part of his official title. He is third cousin to his wife and comes from a royal family; he was born Prince Philip of Greece and Denmark. However, he is not a direct descendant of the reigning House of Windsor and did not inherit the throne; therefore, he is not a king. Philip was coronated (the ceremony of crowning a king or queen) when his wife inherited the throne, but his coronation was much simpler and mostly ceremonial. The same will be true for Middleton when her husband assumes the throne, and she will not be called Queen Catherine. She will be queen consort.

As queen consort, Middleton will not keep the throne if she outlives William; rather, their firstborn child, Prince George of Cambridge, will assume the throne. The same goes for Prince Philip if he outlives Queen Elizabeth II.

Like Queen Elizabeth II's mother, Elizabeth, queen consort to King George VI, Middleton will become queen mother if she outlives her husband. As queen mother, Middleton will still have many of the rights and privileges she enjoyed as queen consort, including living in the royal palaces and maintaining some official and ceremonial importance.

Prince Charles's wait for his turn on the throne has been unexpectedly long. Although he has been groomed for kingship since birth, he has never publicly shown impatience to succeed his mother, instead devoting himself to the expectations of military and public service and deep involvement in charity work.

Prince William has demonstrated a similar patience for his turn on the throne. In fact, Nicholl reported that the gap year he took before heading to college was his way of postponing the many royal duties he would assume after graduating college. In addition to the ups and downs with Middleton, some very public stories from his postcollege life show he perhaps wasn't ready to assume his role as a figurehead for an entire nation. Before and during his military training, he was often seen partying with friends and a string of women who weren't Middleton—even when he was still dating her. Other breaches of royal conduct, such as swimming in the murky moat around an ancient castle on a drunken dare, were reported. For nonroyal young men, this behavior, though not necessarily socially acceptable, is usually chalked up to a phase of immaturity that passes with age. For a prince and future king, however, it was headline news. His brother, Harry, had an even more scandalous party-boy reputation, frequently seen carousing in nightclubs and whipping up controversy one Halloween in a Nazi uniform costume.

The two nonroyal duchesses, Kate Middleton and American actress Meghan Markle (pictured here with Princes William and Harry at a World War I armistice anniversary ceremony in November 2018), have changed the face of the royal family.

Fortunately for themselves and for the royal family, both princes settled down after enduring some highly publicized growing pains. They have grown into charming, charitable men who want to move the monarchy forward under their own terms, including marrying women they truly love rather than noble or royal women chosen by the Crown. (This point was demonstrated when neither prince elected to sign a prenuptial agreement—which protects spouses from losing parts of their fortune or properties—before their marriages, against legal advice. Both Middleton and Markle, however, come with their own high net worth.) The princes have inherited their mother's love for charity and good works and enjoy a similar level of the public popularity that Diana did.

WHAT POWER WILL WILLIAM HAVE AS KING?

Britain is a constitutional monarchy in which the reigning king or queen is head of state but has limited executive power. The monarch is commander in chief of the British Armed Forces, appoints all peerages, and grants knighthoods and other honors, but Britain is governed by a prime minister and the representative legislative body, Parliament. The monarch can be consulted on political affairs and offer opinions to the governing bodies, and must approve bills passed by legislature, but has little direct involvement or authority in governance, policy, and legislation. The monarch can appoint a prime minister and refuse requests to dissolve Parliament and call for an election, but Queen Elizabeth II has never exercised either of those powers in her long reign and it's unlikely her heirs will ever have to exercise them.

Since the 1689 English Bill of Rights, passed after a long, bloody civil war between the Parliament and the Crown, British monarchical power has steadily

(continued on the next page)

(continued from the previous page)

declined to involve mostly official state, ceremonial, diplomatic, and some representational duties. The queen, her heirs, and the other members of the royal family largely serve as figureheads for Britain. Though they host foreign heads of state and travel to other countries to meet with political leaders and governing bodies, their role is mostly to represent Britain, not engage in policy. Queen Elizabeth II is famously nonpolitical; she never publicly expresses political opinions, leaving the prime minister to negotiate with foreign rulers and Parliament to exercise the will of the people. Princes Charles, William, and Harry are more outspoken on their political opinions, leaving political experts eager to see what that might mean for the future of the monarchy.

MOVING CLOSER TO POWER

Both fans of country life, the duke and duchess took up residence in Ammer Hall, a country estate in the English county of Norfolk, after their three years in Wales. The estate was an ideal place for the young family to live because Prince William held an actual real-world job in the area as a pilot with the East Anglian Air Ambulance. He was able to be home in the evenings to read bedtime stories to his children, and the local children played with little Prince George at the playground.

As the time approached for Prince George to enroll in school, however, the family moved its official royal household to Kensington Palace in London. (The family still maintains a residence at Ammer Hall and frequently retreats there when they want private family time out of the public eye.)

Following their three years of early wedded life in Wales, the duke and duchess moved to a country estate, Ammer Hall, in East Anglia, where Prince William put his Royal Air Force training to use as an air ambulance pilot.

Prince William and his younger brother have royal apartments and residences across the royal family's multiple palaces, manors, and other properties, and both princes have lived on the Kensington Palace property before. During their marriage, Prince Charles and Princess Diana had an apartment at Kensington Palace (apartments at Kensington are townhouse-type residences with up to twenty rooms), and after their divorce, Princess Diana kept an apartment there. At various times in their premarriage lives, Princes William and Harry lived in cottages or royal rooms at Kensington, which holds sentimental value to them as the former home of their late mother.

The Duke and Duchess of Cambridge have moved their household to Kensington Palace, which holds sentimental value as the former home of their late mother. Here, Princes William and Harry stroll through the palace's Sunken Garden, a memorial to Diana.

"MIXING TRADITION WITH THE MODERN"

Over its four-hundred-year history, Kensington Palace has been expanded into a sprawling compound that includes apartments and cottages to accommodate minor members of the royal family and occasionally the main royal family itself, when necessary (the queen's chief London residence is Buckingham Palace). Although massive and in a posh part of London, Kensington has an inferior reputation to the family's other palaces, due to it being the dumping ground of minor (often elderly) members of the royal family over the years.

After Prince Harry married Markle in May 2018, it seemed Kensington would undergo a transition with Princes William and Harry living on the property with their wives and families and a favorite first cousin, Princess Eugenie. The press and public speculated that the princes—who have both shown an interest in consolidating their royal and charitable duties and maintaining their close friendship—would make Kensington a base of operations rather than managing their many overlapping functions from separate residences and offices scattered across London. In the 2018 *People/TIME* edition, Prince William was quoted as saying the Kensington compound's current composition mixes "tradition with the modern." Indeed, it does—Markle is the first American to marry into the royal family since the 1930s

The Duke and Duchess of Cambridge and Prince Harry hosted US President Barack Obama and First Lady Michelle Obama at Kensington Palace in April 2016.

(Edward VIII, Queen Elizabeth II's uncle, abdicated the throne in 1936 to marry an American socialite). As an actress, Markle brings her own popularity to the already-public royal stage. As the Duke and Duchess of Cambridge combined forces with Prince Harry and his American wife (now the Duke and Duchess of Sussex), the public turned its eyes toward Kensington. However, the princes' fans—who looked forward to seeing the brothers' families grow up together at Kensington—got some bad news following the October 2018 announcement that the

Duchess of Sussex was pregnant. An October 28, 2018, story in the *Times* reported that the brothers' double act was over:

> They have long appeared to be the closest of brothers, bonded in tragedy and an inseparable element in the worldwide appeal of the royal family. Yet the pressures of monarchy, marriage and their diverging royal roles are presenting new challenges for dukes of Cambridge and Sussex. Princes William, 36, and Harry, 34, considered a formal division of their joint royal household, which is based at Kensington Palace, and the creation of separate courts to reflect their increasingly different responsibilities. A source close to William and Harry said: 'The brothers have leant on each other and looked after each other since their mother died. But now they have their own families, they no longer rely on each other as before.'

In late November 2018, Prince Harry and his wife, Meghan, announced that they were moving to Frogmore Cottage on the Windsor estate in early 2019, in preparation for the birth of their first child. Regardless of how the Dukes and Duchesses of Cambridge and Sussex plan to split their households and somehow maintain a presence in one another's lives, Prince William is committed to maintaining

> There'll be a time and a place to bring George up and understand how he fits in the world. But right now, it's just a case of keeping a secure, stable environment around him and showing him as much love as I can as a father."
>
> **—PRINCE WILLIAM**

a sense of peace for his children, including little George, who will one day take the throne. In the 2018 *People/TIME* story, the duke was quoted on raising his royal heir: "There'll be a time and a place to bring George up and understand how he fits in the world. But right now, it's just a case of keeping a secure, stable environment around him and showing him as much love as I can as a father."

CHAPTER 6

LEAVING A LASTING LEGACY

The institution of the British monarchy has roots going back to the time before there was an England, not to mention the powerful and expansive British Empire that rose between the seventeenth and twentieth centuries (and subsequently diminished as many of its colonies, such as America, obtained freedom). Before there was a nation of England, kings and queens reigned over the separate kingdoms that would one day be England, until centuries of conflict unified those kingdoms to produce one unified nation.

OPPOSITION AND INDIFFERENCE

More than a thousand years of war, invasion, colonial expansion, and hard-fought efforts to remain relevant have produced the modern British monarchy. Although the Duke and Duchess of Cambridge and their children have both captivated and charmed the public, giving the royal family a much-needed public relations boost, their futures aren't as solidified as were their royal predecessors'. Legal limitations on the monarch's power and continued moves from member nations to separate from the United Kingdom have diminished the royals' direct influence over the nation with which they're so identified. The Republic of Ireland successfully broke away from the United Kingdom in the early twentieth century, leaving only a small portion of the country (Protestant-heavy Northern Ireland) under the Crown's dominion. In the 2010s, Scotland renewed its centuries-old desire to be free from its southern neighbor—which brought Scotland into the fold after centuries of border conflict, force, and royal marriages—with referendums to leave the United Kingdom. Like its neighbor the Republic of Ireland, Scotland has shown an interest in joining the European Union.

Although members of the royal family cost taxpayers more than $54 million a year for everything from travel expenses to palace upkeep and improvements, they also generate a lot of money for their nation. According to the British tourism agency,

Although the royal family has been criticized for costing British taxpayers money, the royals attract tourists from around the world. Tourist interest in the royal family generates about 770 million US dollars every year.

the royal family generates close to £500 million (about 770 million US dollars) every year in revenue. Visitors from around the world visit palaces and travel to London to see events like royal weddings or just to catch a glimpse of a newborn royal baby.

ROYAL RELEVANCE

Diminished political power isn't the only issue that royals such as the Duke and Duchess of Cambridge face. Within Britain, interest in the royal family is on the decline; according to a May 2018 Reuters story, only a third of British people surveyed were interested in Prince Harry's wedding to Markle.

Much of the interest in both William's and Harry's weddings came from outside Britain, including the United States, but inside the nation in which William will one day sit on the throne, an increasing number of people don't care all that much about the monarchy. Antimonarchist groups protested on the streets of London amid the celebrations for William's wedding in 2011, and many within Britain see the monarchy as an outdated institution that unnecessarily consumes taxpayer dollars and has little to do with the everyday lives of its subjects. According to Reuters, more than half of those surveyed believed the royal family itself, not the taxpayers, should be responsible for costs like the weddings of its family members and the police that those events require. Only 37 percent want Charles to succeed to the throne upon his mother's death, with most people preferring someone else, like Prince William, take the throne. An antimonarchist quoted in Reuters said the poll shows "a very clear picture of a nation disinterested and apathetic about the royal family."

Antimonarchist groups emphasize everything from a 2007 controversy surrounding Prince Harry's alleged shooting of rare, legally protected birds to a near doubling of the queen's income in 2017 (bringing her income to about 104 million US dollars a year) in their efforts to undermine the royal family. Although global fascination with the royal family remains strong, Charles and his heirs may have to reckon with public demand for an even greater reduction in the monarchy's role—especially the family's taxpayer-supported functions.

Ahead of the October 2018 wedding of Princess Eugenie, William's and Harry's first cousin, an October 8, 2018, *YAHOO!* news headline made it clear the British public is also displeased with taxpayer money going to lavish royal weddings and ceremonies. Although the princess's wedding ceremony and related celebrations were mostly paid for by Eugenie's father, Prince Andrew, the Duke of York, the British public paid for nearly £2 million (about 2.5 million US dollars) in security costs like additional police and road closures. (The $32 million—about £25 million—in security costs for the Duke and Duchess of Cambridge's 2011 wedding was also paid for with taxpayer money). Ninety percent of people polled in Britain said they did not believe the public should bear the expense for the princess's wedding, especially since Eugenie had given up her official royal duties (meaning she no longer works on behalf of the British people).

The princes are aware that their public is wary of the monarchy. A June 22, 2017, *Vanity Fair* article discussed comments from Prince Harry, one of the royal family's most popular members, that suggest the current and future

Charity is the emphasis for the new generation of royals. The Duke and Duchess of Cambridge, pictured here with Prince Harry at the April 2017 opening of a state-funded media school, are patrons or supporters of dozens of charities.

royal generations are reluctant. The prince said he does not believe anyone in the royal family wants to be king or queen, but all will do their duties nonetheless. William is less direct than his more outspoken younger brother, having been groomed for kingly restraint since birth, but his gap year and his voluntary additional military service point toward a young man who was not yet ready to fully step into the royal shoes. Prince Charles has said his reign will be a slimmed-down version of his mother's; indicators of his public life today show he may place more emphasis on charitable efforts than on ceremonial functions and the traditional precedents that govern Queen Elizabeth II's family.

REMAINING RELEVANT

Many chroniclers of the royal family place an emphasis on one word: survival. Queen Elizabeth II has dedicated her life to serving as the monarch, a promise she made when she was crowned. She has never given a press interview. She keeps her political opinions to herself and to the circle of governmental officials with whom she's legally allowed to share them. She requires a certain amount of decorum from her family members and has only recently bended to their desires to marry outsiders (though both Princes William and Harry still had to get her permission to marry outside the aristocracy). Though it took the queen decades to allow "common" outsiders into her family, it's those outsiders who have already

Though Middleton (*right*) and Markle (*fourth from right*) have introduced a more relaxed influence into the royal family, the family is still governed by the queen's rules regarding everything from who stands where in pictures to how to dress and behave in public.

shown they're a force for good in the royals' future.

OUTSIDE INFLUENCE

Upon returning from a month-long trip abroad when his son was just a boy, Prince Philip was once photographed greeting his young son, Charles, by doing nothing more than tousling his hair. Charles himself instructed Princes William and Harry not to cry at their mother's funeral.

William's public affection for his wife and his children heralds a new way of living as a family, and he openly credits his wife's warmer, more easygoing family for showing him an alternative to what he experienced as a child. A January 8, 2016, E!News story put it this way: "Family life didn't have to be made up of formal dinners with butlers and servants and rules and regulations."

Both Middleton and Markle have been credited with introducing a new and modern element to the monarchy and with changing the face of the institution forever. Both women bring a practical sensibility and warmth that stems from growing up outside the British aristocracy. Although they're both famously beautiful and fashionable, their friendly personalities and relatable backgrounds make them more accessible to the everyday public. Although Middleton may be technically the first non-noble to marry a throne-bound Windsor, she and Markle are not the firsts in the family to find their way into the public's heart.

IN DIANA'S FOOTSTEPS

William's public affection for his wife and family is not the only indicator of the prince's shift toward a new status quo for the royal family. Along with his younger brother, William has spoken publicly about mental health issues, pointing to his mother's struggles with depression and his own depression after his mother's untimely death. Mental health is actually among the most important issues in which the duke and his wife have involved themselves through Heads Together, a program of the princes' combined philanthropic organization, The Royal Foundation.

DUKES AND DUCHESSES COMBINE FORCES

In 2009, realizing they could be more effective if they combined their philanthropic efforts, Princes William and Harry began the Royal Foundation with their own money. The foundation became operational when Middleton joined in 2011 after marrying William, and Markle joined the organization when she became engaged to Harry in 2018. The foundation's programs fall under four main areas: mental health, wildlife and conservation, young people, and the armed forces community.

> "We feel passionately that, working closely together with those who contribute to our Foundation, we can help to make a long-lasting and tangible difference."
>
> **—PRINCE WILLIAM**

Through the foursome's own contributions as patrons (the princes give their salaries, such as what they make through the military, directly to charity) and through fund-raising, the foundation raises millions of dollars a year for a diverse range of charities and services. In Penny Junor's book, *Prince William: The Man Who Will Be King*, the duke said, "We feel passionately that, working closely together with those who contribute to our Foundation, we can help to make a long-lasting and tangible difference."

LEAVING A LEGACY

The monarchy's future lies in the hands of the Duke and Duchess of Cambridge and the Duke and Duchess of Sussex. William and Middleton have done a great deal to soften the public's perception of the royal family by experiencing trials, like relationship problems, that everyday people experience—and by prevailing despite the challenges they've so often faced. Their home-cooked meals and hands-on family life make them easier to understand for ordinary people, who appreciate the couple's commitment to leading as ordinary and peaceful a life as possible for their children's sakes. Although a young Prince William went to his first day of school under the glare of the media's flashing cameras, Middleton insisted no press get near Prince George on his first day of school. She often transports her children to school herself and has been photographed sitting in London traffic on her way to drop Prince George off at school. The children see their nonroyal grandparents just as much as they see their royal grandparents, and Middleton has instituted a new tradition of both families meeting for Christmas. And, although Middleton and Markle will always live, to some degree, in Princess Diana's shadow, they've shown strength of will against the old guard of the royal family without being disrespectful. This transformation will serve the current and future generations of the royal family well by permitting them greater freedom to permit positive outside influences. It will also help the royal family continue to do what it always does: survive.

Through their children, the duke and duchess have already left a legacy. But their legacy certainly does not begin and end with the heirs they've produced: through their foundation, they oversee and fund dozens of charities that carry out services and support for everything from wounded soldiers to victims of cyberbullying to mental health awareness and

> Leaving a lasting legacy is vital to maintaining the royal family's relevance. In endeavoring to leave a legacy, Prince William and Middleton follow closely in Diana's philanthropic footsteps, often visiting sick children and working closely with their many charities.

assistance. Their generosity has helped thousands, and both dukes and duchesses are spotted on the charity trail on a regular basis, whether it's playing with sick children through a medical institution they support or hosting a prominent forum on reducing the stigma of mental illness.

What the monarchy will look like by the time Prince William inherits the throne is uncertain. He and his brother know the royal family has been unpopular in the past and that the institution itself is opposed by some of their subjects. They also know that the monarchy is an institution for good, which they endeavor to prove every day through making a massively positive difference in the lives of others who weren't born into the privilege they were.

William and Kate are part of what is perhaps the most famous family in the world. The couple has set a new standard for the face of the British royal family. They're not just figureheads: together, they're a shining symbol of the future and of unity for their nation.

1982 Catherine "Kate" Middleton is born on January 8, in Reading, England. Prince William is born on June 21 in London, England.

2001 Prince William and Middleton meet at University of St. Andrews in September.

2002 Middleton catches Prince William's eye in a college fashion show, and the two later become off-campus roommates.

2003 Middleton and Prince William move into a private estate in the town of St. Andrews.

2004 The *Sun* makes Middleton and Prince William's relationship public with a skiing photo.

2005 Middleton and Prince William graduate from the University of St. Andrews.

2006 Prince William completes military training.

2007 Middleton and Prince William separate for several months.

2008 Princes William and Harry found the Royal Foundation.

2010 Middleton and Prince William get engaged in October and formally announce their engagement in November.

2011 Middleton and Prince William get married on April 29 and spend the next three years living in Wales.

2013 Prince George, the couple's first child, is born on July 22.

2014 The duke and duchess move to Ammer House in Norfolk.

2015 Princess Charlotte, the couple's second child, is born on May 2.

2017 The duke and duchess move their household to Kensington Palace.

2018 Prince Louis, the couple's third child, is born on April 23.

aristocracy The highest class in some societies, often consisting of nobility.

baron Also called "Lord" in Britain, the lowest order of British nobility.

commoner A person without rank or title.

countess The wife of a count or earl.

duchess The wife of a duke; duchesses hold territories called duchies.

duke A man who holds the highest noble title in a peerage system; dukes hold territories called duchies.

dynasty In certain societies, such as those with royal families, a line of hereditary rulers.

earl A British nobleman.

fascinator A headpiece that is decorative and made out of a lightweight material.

heir apparent A person who has a claim to take over a role.

House of Hanover The German royal line that gave birth to the current British royal family.

House of Windsor The reigning royal house of the United Kingdom and its commonwealths.

investiture They day on which the queen or a member of the royal family awards an honor or rank on someone.

lady In certain societies, a woman of nobility.

monarch The sovereign head of state, such as a king or a queen.

parliament A legislative body; in the United Kingdom, it consists of the sovereign (the queen), the House of Lords, and the House of Commons.

peerage The class of people, called peers, who have hereditary or noble titles.

prime minister The head of elected government in some countries.

primogeniture A system in which the firstborn child has the right of succession.

royal The status of a king or queen and members of his or her family.

Saxe-Coburg-Gotha The original family name for the current British dynasty.

succession The process in which a person inherits a title, position, land, or office.

territorial designation The system in which members of the peerage system are linked to a specific place.

The British Royal Family
Buckingham Palace
London SW1A 1AA
United Kingdom
+44 (0)20 7930 4832
Website: https://www.royal.uk
Facebook: @TheBritishMonarchy
Twitter: @RoyalFamily
The official website of the royal family gives comprehensive information on the family's and monarchy's history; biographical information on members of the royal family; and details about their roles, responsibilities, and charity work.

Government of Canada—Monarchy and the Crown
Website: https://www.canada.ca
Facebook and Twitter: @TheCrownCa
Canada is a constitutional monarchy and one of the British commonwealths. The Government of Canada's website offers information on how the British royal family stays involved in Canada and how the monarch remains a part of Canada's national identity.

Prince of Wales Official Website
Clarence House
London SW1A 1BA
United Kingdom
Website: https://www.princeofwales.gov.uk

Twitter: @ClarenceHouse
The official site of the Prince of Wales and the
    Duchess of Cornwall provides royal family
    biographies, descriptions of royal duties, and
    current and historical information on the royals.

Royal Foundation
Kensington Palace
Palace Green
London W8 4PU
United Kingdom
Email: info@royalfoundation.com
Website: https://www.royalfoundation.com
Instagram and Twitter: @KensingtonRoyal
The Royal Foundation is the combined charity
    organization for the Duke and Duchess of
    Cambridge and the Duke and Duchess of
    Sussex. The foundation's four main charitable
    themes are mental health, wildlife and
    conservation, young people, and the armed
    forces community. The website provides
    information on its specific charities.

Royal Historical Society
23-25 Gower Street
Kings Cross
London WC1E 6BT
United Kingdom
+44 (0)20 7387 7532
Email: enquiries@royalhistsoc.org

Website: https://royalhistsoc.org
Facebook and Twitter: @RoyalHistSoc
Founded in 1868, the Royal Historical Society
    works with professional historians on the
    scholarly study of history, including the history
    of British royals.

Royal Society of Canada
Walter House
282 Somerset West
Ottawa, ON K2P 0J6
Canada
(613) 991-6990
Website: http://rsc-src.ca
Facebook and Twitter: @RSCTheAcademies
Established by Parliament in 1883, the Society
    is an organization of scholars, artists, and
    scientists. Modeled on the Royal Society of
    London, the Royal Society of Canada was
    founded by a British nobleman and provides
    intellectual leadership.

Diemer, Lauren, and Heather Kissock. *Prince William and Kate Middleton* (Remarkable People). New York, NY: AV² by Weigl, 2014.

Editors of *LIFE*. *The New Royals: Grace, Purpose, Promise*. New York, NY: LIFE Books, 2017.

Editors of *People*. *Princess Kate: Royal Mom, Future Queen: Inside Her Life Today*. New York, NY: People Books, 2016.

Edwards, Anne. *Matriarch: Queen Mary and the House of Windsor*. Lanham, MD: Rowman & Littlefield Publishers, 2015.

Hoare, Jerry, and Ellen Labrecque. *Who Was Princess Diana?* New York, NY: Scholastic, 2017.

Hunter, Nick. *Catherine, Duchess of Cambridge*. Chicago, IL: Capstone Raintree, 2014.

Jackson, Chris. *Modern Monarchy: The British Royal Family Today*. New York, NY: Rizzoli, 2018.

Junor, Penny. *Prince William: The Man Who Will Be King*. New York, NY: Pegasus Books, 2012.

Lewis, Brenda Ralph. *The Untold History of the Kings and Queens of England*. New York, NY: Cavendish Square, 2017.

New York Times editorial staff. *Royal Couples: Harry and Meghan Markle, William and Kate Middleton, and Charles and Diana*. New York, NY: New York Times Educational Publishing, 2019.

Nicholl, Katie. *Kate: The Future Queen*. New York, NY: Weinstein Books, 2015.

Novis, Constance, and Helen Fewster. *Queen Elizabeth II and the Royal Family*. New York, NY: DK Publishing, 2015.

Ribke, Simone T. *William and Kate: The Prince and Princess*. New York, NY: Children's Press, 2016.

Sherman, Jill. *Prince Harry & Meghan* (Gateway Biographies). Minneapolis, MN: Lerner Publications, 2019.

Shoup, Kate. *Kate Middleton: From Commoner to Duchess of Cambridge*. New York, NY: Cavendish Square, 2015.

Starkey, David. *Crown and Country: A History of England through the Monarchy*. New York, NY: HarperPress, 2011.

ABC News. "Prince William and Kate Middleton Talk about the Moment, the Ring, Children." ABC News. November 16, 2010. https://abcnews.go.com/Entertainment/prince-william-kate-middleton-interview-transcript/story?id=12163826.

Alden, Chris. "Britain's Monarchy." *Guardian*, May 16, 2002. https://www.theguardian.com/world/2002/may/16/qanda.jubilee.

Barr, Sabrina. "This Is the Royal Title the Duchess of Cambridge Will Receive When Prince William Becomes King." *Independent*, September 3, 2018. https://www.independent.co.uk/life-style/kate-middleton-royal-title-queen-prince-william-king-duchess-cambridge-queen-a8520356.html.

British Broadcasting Network. "New Rules on Royal Succession Come into Force." BBC, March 26, 2015. https://www.bbc.com/news/uk-32073399.

British Broadcasting Network. "Prince Charles and Lady Diana Spencer's Wedding." BBC History. Retrieved September 9, 2018. https://www.bbc.co.uk/history/events.

British Broadcasting Network. "Q&A: Queen's Wedding Decision." BBC, February 23, 2005. http://news.bbc.co.uk/2/hi/uk_news/4289417.stm.

British Royal Family. *Charities and Patronages*. Retrieved September 12, 2018. https://www.royal.uk/charities-and-patronages.

British Royal Family. *The Royal Family*. Retrieved September 12, 2018. https://www.royal.uk /royal-family.

Bromley, Melanie. "Kate Middleton at 34: From Normal Girl to Future Queen, How She Managed to Change the Monarchy Forever." E!News, January 8, 2016. https://www.eonline .com/fr/news/729274/kate-middleton-at-33 -from-normal-girl-to-future-queen-how-she -managed-to-change-the-monarchy-forever.

Butan, Christina. "The Royals: The Story of the Windsors Today." *People,* August 17, 2018. https://people.com/royals/the-windsors-today -people-celebrates-the-royal-family-in-new -special-edition.

Daily Telegraph Reporter. "Kate Middleton 'First Laid Eyes on Prince William as a 10-Year-Old Schoolgirl.'" *Telegraph,* November 27, 2010. https://www.telegraph.co.uk/news/uknews /royal-wedding/8162448/Kate-Middleton-first -laid-eyes-on-Prince-William-as-a-10-year-old -schoolgirl.html.

Decker, Megan. "Everything You Need to Know about Prince William and Kate Middleton's Children." *Harper's Bazaar*, April 27, 2018. https://www.harpersbazaar.com/celebrity /latest/a19811611/kate-middleton-prince -william-royal-kids.

Gibson, Kelsie. "Prince William on Princess Diana: 'I Still Miss My Mother Every Day.'" POPSUGAR,

August 31, 2016. https://www.popsugar
.com/celebrity/Prince-William-Quotes-About
-Princess-Diana-August-2016-42276792.

Gonzales, Erica. "People Want Royals, Not
Taxpayers, to Cover the $2.5 Million Security
Bill for Princess Eugenie's Wedding." *Harper's
Bazaar*, September 28, 2018. https://www
.harpersbazaar.com/celebrity/latest
/a23507002/princess-eugenie-wedding
-petition-security-cost.

Gordon, Bryony. "The Duchess of Cambridge:
Why We All Need to Open Up about Mental
Health." *Telegraph*, May 17, 2016. https://
www.telegraph.co.uk/women/life/the-duchess
-of-cambridge-why-we-all-need-to-open-up
-about-mental.

Grossbart, Sarah. "Secret Getaways, Splits and
That Fashion Show: The Early Days of Prince
William and Kate Middleton's Romance."
E!News, April 29, 2018. https://www.eonline
.com/news/930571/secret-getaways-splits
-and-that-fashion-show-the-early-days-of
-prince-william-and-kate-middleton-s
-romance.

Halleman, Caroline. "Who Will Pay for Prince
Harry and Meghan Markle's Wedding?" *Town
& Country*, May 17, 2018. https://www
.townandcountrymag.com/society/tradition
/a15906479/prince-harry-meghan-markle
-royal-wedding-cost-who-pays.

Harris, Stephanie Ayako Karaki. "British Public Is 'Sick' of Princess Eugenie's Wedding." YAHOO!, October 8, 2018. https://www .yahoo.com/news/princess-eugenies-wedding -british-public-sick-royal-family-104327528 .html.

Junor, Penny. *Prince William: The Man Who Will Be King.* New York, NY: Pegasus Books, 2013.

Katz, Gregory, and Martin Benedyk. "From Pit to Palace: Kate's Coal Mining Ancestry." *Washington Post,* March 3, 2011. http://www .washingtonpost.com/wp-dyn/content /article/2011/03/03/AR2011030301599.html.

Khazan, Olga. "Is the British Royal Family Worth the Money?" *Atlantic,* July 23, 2013. https:// www.theatlantic.com/international/archive /2013/07/is-the-british-royal-family-worth -the-money/278052.

Leodis: A Photographic Archive of Leeds. "Headingley Castle." Retrieved September 12, 2018. http://www.leodis.net/display. aspx?resourceIdentifier=9113&DISPLAY=FULL.

Marie Claire. "This Is How Prince William Proposed to Kate Middleton." *Marie Claire,* May 3, 2017. https://www.marieclaire.co.uk.

McCabe, Joanne. "Royal Wedding Live YouTube Stream Watched by 72m." *Metro,* May 9, 2011. https://metro.co.uk/2011/05/09/royal -wedding-live-youtube-stream-watched-by -72million-people-4558.

Nicholl, Katie. *Kate: The Future Queen*. New York, NY: Weinstein Books, 2015.

Nicholl, Katie. "Kate Middleton's Royal Catwalk." *Vanity Fair*, September 2012. https://www.vanityfair.com/style/2012/09/kate-middletons-married-life-house-facials.

Nicholl, Katie. "Prince Harry's Shocking Comments and the Future of the Monarchy." *Vanity Fair,* June 22, 2017. https://www.vanityfair.com/style/2017/06/prince-harry-monarchy-comments.

Nicholl, Katie. "Wills and the Real Girl." *Vanity Fair*, November 4, 2010. https://www.vanityfair.com/news/2010/12/william-and-kate-201012.

Nikkah, Roya. "Princes Harry and William to Call It a Day for Their Double Act." *Times*, October 28, 2018. https://www.thetimes.co.uk/article/princes-harry-and-william-to-call-it-a-day-for-their-double-act-3pq5h0xgc.

Power, Gabriel. "Inside Kensington Palace: William and Kate's London Family Home." *Week*, June 6, 2018. http://www.theweek.co.uk/81070/inside-kensington-palace-william-and-kate-s-london-family-home.

Rayner, Gordon. "William and Kate Make Nostalgic Trip to Anglesey to Mark End of RAF Search and Rescue Force." *Telegraph*, February 18, 2016. https://www.telegraph.co.uk/news/uknews/kate-middleton/12163037/William

-and-Kate-make-nostalgic-trip-to-Anglesey-to
-mark-end-of-RAF-Search-and-Rescue-Force
.html.

Read, Carly. "Kate Says Prince William DIDN'T
Feature on her Bedroom Wall—But Admits
Who Did." *Express*, September 7, 2018.
https://www.express.co.uk/news/royal
/1014584/prince-william-kate-middleton
-interview-bedroom-wall-poster-levis.

Shoup, Kate. *Kate Middleton: From Commoner
to Duchess of Cambridge*. New York, NY:
Cavendish Square, 2015.

Smith, David. "Family Plea to be Left Alone after
Kate's Split with Prince." *Guardian*, April 14,
2007. https://www.theguardian.com/uk/2007
/apr/15/monarchy.davidsmith1.

Smout, Alistair. "Two-thirds of Brits Not Interested
in Royal Wedding: Poll." Reuters, May 14,
2018. https://www.reuters.com/article
/us-britain-royals-wedding-poll.

Sykes, Tom. "Harry and Meghan to Move Into Flat
Next to William and Kate, with Connecting
Door." Daily Beast, May 8, 2018. https://www
.thedailybeast.com/harry-and-meghan-to
-move-into-flat-next-to-william-and-kate-with
-connecting-door.

Tieck, Sarah. *Kate Middleton: Real-Life Princess*.
Minneapolis, MN: ABDO Publishing, 2012.

Van Gilder Cooke, Sonia. "First Come, First
Crowned: The British Monarchy Gets Modern."

TIME, October 31, 2011. http://content.time
.com/time/world/article/0,8599,2098162,00
.html.

Weinstein, Shelli. "Kate Middleton Delivers a
Passionate Speech about Children's Mental
Health." *TV Guide*, November 18, 2015.
https://www.tvguide.com/news/kate-middleton
-childrens-mental-health-speech.

ABOUT THE AUTHOR

Angie Timmons is a writer and an ardent student of history, especially British history. Her works include *The Rape of Nanjing* and books on the Cold War and World War II. Timmons's background in news and politics has contributed to her interest in how the current royal family has transformed to remain relevant and strong while maintaining some of its historical traditions.

PHOTO CREDITS

Cover Scott Barbour/Getty Images; p. 7 AFP/Getty Images; p. 11 David Levenson/Hulton Archive/Getty Images; p. 14 Anwar Hussein/Hulton Archive/Getty Images; pp. 17, 60 Julian Parker/UK Press/Getty Images; p. 19 Richard Baker/In Pictures/Getty Images; p. 21 Adam Butler - PA Images/Getty Images; p. 27 Handout/WireImage/Getty Images; p. 31 Bletchley Park Trust/SSPL/Getty Images; p. 33 Historic Images/Alamy Stock Photo; p. 35 Getty Images; pp. 36, 70, 73, 84 WPA Pool/Getty Images; p. 40 UK Press/Getty Images; p. 43 fashionpix/Alamy Stock Photo; p. 46 Handout/Getty Images; p. 48 (both) Michael Dunlea/AFP/Getty Images; p. 51 Adrian Dennis/AFP/Getty Images; pp. 54, 86 Chris Jackson/Getty Images; p. 56 Ben Stansall/AFP/Getty Images; p. 62 Dominic Lipinski/AFP/Getty Images; p. 74 Karwai Tang/WireImage/Getty Images; p. 76 Official White House Photo by Pete Souza; p. 81 George Pimentel/WireImage/Getty Images; p. 90 Eamonn M. McCormack/Getty Images; additional interior pages design elements Levchenko Ilia/Shutterstock.com (light streaks), Shmizla/Shutterstock.com (dot pattern), Romeo Budai/EyeEm/Getty Images (sparkle backgrounds).

Design: Nicole Russo-Duca; Senior Editor: Kathy Kuhtz Campbell; Photo Researcher: Nicole Reinholdt